W9-AXJ-330

Discovering Science

The House that Science Built

Michael Pollard

Facts On File Publications
New York, New York ● Oxford, England

Contents

Photographic credits

t = top   b = bottom   l = left   r = right   c = center

6*l*, 6*r*, 7, 9*t*, 9*b* ZEFA; 16 Chris Fairclough; 20 South American Pictures; 30 Biophotos/NHPA; 31 Frank Lane Picture Library; 32 Oxford Scientific Films; 34 David Redfern Photography; 36 Sony/Dawson Strange; 37, 38, 41 ZEFA

Illustrations by George Fryer/Linden Artists, Sebastian Quigley/Linden Artists, Sallie Alane Reason

Discovering Science/The House That Science Built

Copyright © BLA Publishing Limited 1987

First published in the United States of America by Facts on File, Inc. 460 Park Avenue South, New York, New York 10016.

Library of Congress Catalog Card Number:
87-80099

Designed and produced by BLA Publishing Limited, East Grinstead, Sussex, England.

A member of the **Ling Kee Group**
LONDON · HONG KONG · TAIPEI · SINGAPORE · NEW YORK

Printed in Italy by New Interlitho

10 9 8 7 6 5 4 3 2 1

NOTE TO THE READER: while you are reading this book you will notice that certain words appear in **bold type**. This is to indicate a word listed in the Glossary on page 45. This glossary gives brief explanations of words which may be new to you.

Science and the home

Our homes are important to all of us. They give us shelter. Homes are where we eat and sleep, and spend much of our time. Most of us try to make our homes as comfortable as we can. Science helps us to do this in many ways. It helps us to keep our homes warm and clean. It also makes them easier to run.

Using science

The use of science is sometimes called **technology**. It helps builders to build strong, safe homes. We have light or heat just by pressing a switch. We have cold or hot water whenever we want it.

Some homes are full of machines. They help us to do jobs around the house like cooking and cleaning. Technology also gives us entertainment at home such as radio and TV.

All these machines need **energy** to make them work. Most of this energy comes to our homes in the form of **electricity**.

Cables link each house with a power station. Inside the house, cables take electric current to each room. We can switch on, or plug in, to make each machine work. All this energy in the home has to be paid for. It is one of the main costs of running a home.

Where do you live?

We all live in different types of houses. Some houses are on one floor. They do not need stairs. Other houses have two or more floors. Apartments are built one on top of another, in a block. Houses are often joined on one or both sides to other houses. You can see many different types of houses in the picture. Can you see one that looks like your home?

In the country

In the country, there is more space. The houses are often wide apart. The nearest neighbor may live a long distance away. Many people in the country work on the land. Their houses may have yards, stables and other buildings for farm animals.

Children who live in the country often have a long way to go to school. In some parts of the world, there are no schools for them. So they have to work at home. In parts of Australia, the lessons come to them by radio.

▲ In the farm lands of Canada families live far apart from each other.

▲ Some houses in Bristol are nearly 200 years old. Now they are used as apartments.

Villages and small towns

People who live in small towns and villages often lead a **community** life. They know each other well, and share common interests. Sometimes, several **generations** of a family live in the same place. In some parts of the world, such as Africa and India, families that are related may share the same house.

Most houses in small towns and villages have gardens. These can be used for children to play in, and for growing vegetables and flowers.

In the city

Four out of ten people in the world live in cities. People go to cities to find work. There is a shortage of land in cities and they become crowded.

Some people live in flats or apartment

▲ These are apartment blocks near Hamburg, West Germany. The buildings are divided into apartments. Families who live on the top floor have a good view. But they are further from the stores and playground than those who live on the ground floor.

blocks. Others live in houses away from the center in the **suburbs** of the city. Few of those who live in the city have gardens or space around their homes. That is why most cities have parks and public gardens. People can go there to walk or play.

Almost all the cities in the world are still growing. There are not enough new houses. It is hard to find somewhere to live. In some cities, people who cannot find a home build their own. They use any **materials** they can find. They build on spare land at the edges of a city. Sometimes these groups of rough houses are called **shanty towns**.

Houses around the world

A house protects the people who live in it. It keeps them dry in wet weather. It keeps them warm in cold weather and cool in hot weather. Houses are **designed** to suit the climate of the place where they are built. They may have to stand up to strong winds, heavy rain or snow.

Sites for houses are chosen with care. Water must drain away when it rains, or the houses will be flooded. If the ground is too soft, the house may sink in the ground. Great care must be taken in parts of the world where there are **earthquakes**. Houses there must be built on strong frames.

▼ In hot countries, houses have small windows with wooden shutters. Can you see the wind tower?

Houses in hot climates

In countries with hot, dry climates most houses have flat roofs. They do not need **pitched** roofs to carry rain water away. The main need is for the houses to keep cool in the daytime, when the sun beats down.

Houses are built close together so that they shade each other from the sun. The windows are small. They have wooden shutters instead of glass. The shutters are opened in the daytime. Then air can flow through and cool the house. Sometimes there is a wind tower with open windows. This allows the warm air to escape from the top of the house. Then cooler air can flow in at the ground level.

▲ In the Alps, the roofs of houses may be covered with snow throughout the winter.

Houses in cold climates

In cold climates, houses are built to keep warmth in and the cold out. They are often built of wood. Wood is a good **insulator**. Wooden houses have an outer and an inner 'skin' of wood, with a gap in between.

The roofs of houses in cold climates are steeply pitched. This lets most of the snow slide off. If it did not, the weight of the snow could make the roof collapse. Some snow stays on the roof. This helps to keep the heat of the house in.

Bad housing

We all want to live in good houses. In many parts of the world, people have very poor housing. Their houses are too small and cramped. The houses may be old and in poor condition. Some may not have a supply of water. They may be hard to keep warm and dry.

There is poor housing of this kind in most cities. Areas of poor housing are called slums. Shanty towns are slums of a different kind. The houses there have been built badly by the people who live in them. Too many people in the world have to live in bad houses.

▼ There are still shanty towns like this one in some parts of the world.

9

Building materials

Houses are built of many different materials. In countries like Canada and Norway, there are plenty of trees. Houses there are often made of wood. In rocky parts of the world, builders sometimes use stone when it is near at hand. Wood and stone are natural materials. They have to be sawn or cut to the right shape and size.

Many building materials are made in factories. They are made in fixed sizes. This makes building quicker and easier. Bricks are made of clay, in brickworks. Building blocks are made of **concrete**.

Many other materials are used to build houses. Clay pipes are used for drains. Glass is needed for the windows. Metal can be used for window frames. Plastic pipes are often used to take away water.

Wood

In most houses, wood is used to make part of the frame. Wooden **trusses** support the roof. Wooden beams called **joists** hold up the ceilings and floors. Doors, window frames and floors can be made of wood. Wood is easy to cut and shape, and to fix into place.

Sometimes wood is sawn up and the wood chips are glued together to make panels and boards. These are used for doors and floors. This material is called **chipboard**.

Stone

Stone is hard to work with and few houses are made of stone today. Some houses are given a stone facing. This is a thin layer of stone used to decorate houses.

Clay

Clay is used to make bricks, tiles and pipes. Damp clay is first put into moulds to give it shape. Then it is dried and heated in a brick kiln. It bakes hard to make a very good building material. It is strong and waterproof. It also resists fire, and the dust and dirt of city air.

Clay pipes used to carry water are glazed on the inside. They are given a shiny coating like cups and saucers. Because of this, water runs through them without escaping.

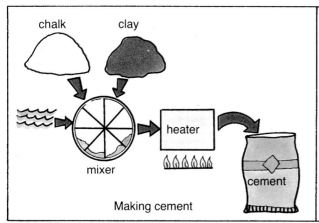

Making cement

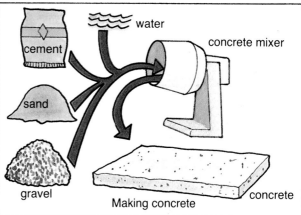

Making concrete

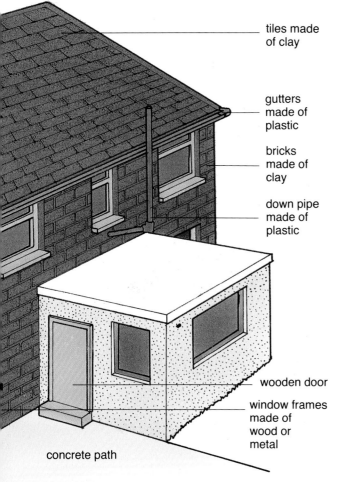

tiles made of clay

gutters made of plastic

bricks made of clay

down pipe made of plastic

wooden door

window frames made of wood or metal

concrete path

Sand and cement

Cement is a mixture of limestone and clay. When it is dried and burned it becomes a whitish powder. When mixed with water and sand, it is called **mortar**. Mortar is used to join bricks and other building materials together.

Cement and sand are also used to make concrete. Gravel or other small stones are added to the mixture. When it dries, it makes a hard surface for roads, paths and walls.

Steel

Many modern houses and larger buildings are built on steel frames. Steel **girders** are also used as joists to hold up floors and ceilings.

Plastics

Pipes made of plastics are cheaper than those made of clay. They are easy to cut and fix. Many modern houses have rain water gutters and down pipes made of plastics. They can also be used under the ground for water and gas supply.

11

Designing houses

The place where a new house is built is called a building **site**. The site must be close to the main **services**. These are water, drains and gas or electricity. They are sometimes called the mains.

The **architect** designs the house and draws the **plans**. It is his or her job to make sure that the new house will look good and will be good to live in. The design must fit in with other houses nearby. When it is finished, the house must be just right for the people who are going to live there.

Surveying the site

The site is **surveyed** before the building work starts. The surveyor measures the site and works out slopes and dips in the land.

The surveyor uses a **theodolite** to work out the levels. This is a kind of telescope on legs. The telescope can be moved up or down, and from side to side. The surveyor looks through it at a marked pole to find out if the land is level. When the site survey is finished, a map called a site plan is drawn.

▼ Before the builders start their work, a surveyor has to measure up the site. Pegs are put in the ground to mark out the position of the house. The surveyor uses a theodolite to measure heights and angles. He tells the builder how much soil must be moved to make the site level.

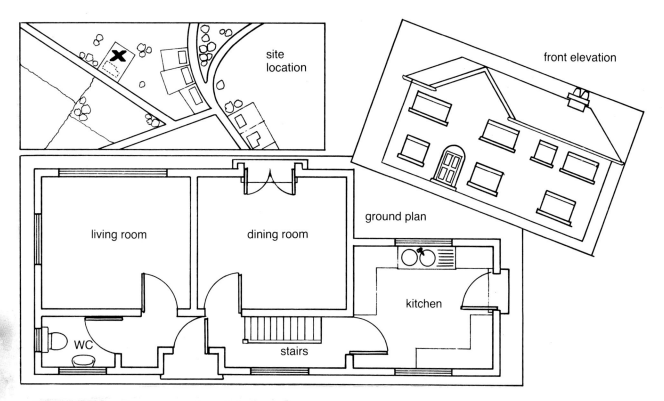

site location

front elevation

ground plan

living room

dining room

kitchen

WC

stairs

The architect's plans

Now the architect can make plans. One plan shows how the house will fit on to the site. Another plan shows what the houses will look like from above. There is a plan for each floor showing how the rooms are to be arranged. Drawings that show what each side of the house will look like are called **elevations**.

The architect's plans show the builder how to build the house. They show where the doors and windows are to go. They show how the mains will connect up with the house. The plans also tell the builder what kind of bricks and tiles to use. The architect has to visit the site quite often to check that the builders are doing the work correctly.

Building houses

The first people to do work on a building site are the earth-moving gang. They use bulldozers and diggers to level the ground where the house will stand. Dump trucks take away any soil that is not needed. Then trenches are dug leading to the house site. These will carry the main water pipes and power cables.

When the site is level, posts are driven into the ground. They mark the corners of the house. Now the builder brings in a site hut to store tools and the plans. Trucks arrive with bricks and timber. Building is about to start.

▼ **Laying the foundations.** A wooden frame is put down. Concrete is poured in up to the level of the pegs. When the concrete has set hard, the wooden frame is removed.

Laying the foundations

Every building must have firm **foundations**. These make the hard base on which it stands. A large building stands on steel or concrete piles driven deep into the ground. The foundations of a house are made of concrete. This is first laid in trenches dug out where the walls will go.

When the concrete has set hard, bricks or concrete blocks are laid on it up to the level of the ground floor. Now concrete is poured in to make the floor foundations. It is carefully leveled, and left to set hard.

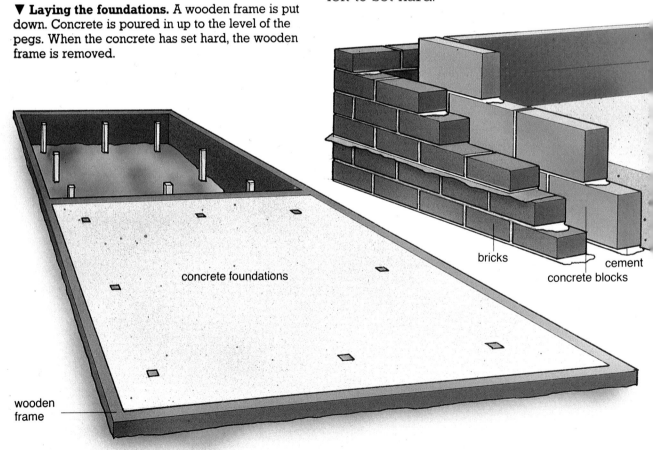

bricks

cement

concrete blocks

concrete foundations

wooden frame

Building the walls

Most houses are built with **cavity walls**. The cavity is a space between two layers of bricks or blocks. Larger blocks are usually used for the inside layer. This will not show when the house is finished. Bricks, or blocks with timber **cladding**, are used for the outer layer. The bricks are laid on mortar made of sand and cement. The bricklayer has to make sure that each layer of bricks is level.

▼ **Building the walls.** A cavity wall is built around the concrete foundations. There are concrete blocks on the inside, then a cavity. Bricks are laid around the outside of the cavity.

The roof

When the walls are finished, carpenters fix the roof and floors. In small houses the joists holding up the ceilings and floors are made of wood. In large buildings, they are steel girders.

The framework of the roof is made of wood. The main frames are called trusses. They are fixed in place first. The inside of the roof is covered with felt. Then strips of wood, called **battens**, are nailed across the **rafters**, and over the felt. Finally, tiles are nailed to the battens, so that each tile overlaps the tile below it.

▼ **Making the roof.** When the outside walls are completed, the roof trusses and joists are put in place. Then the roof is made.

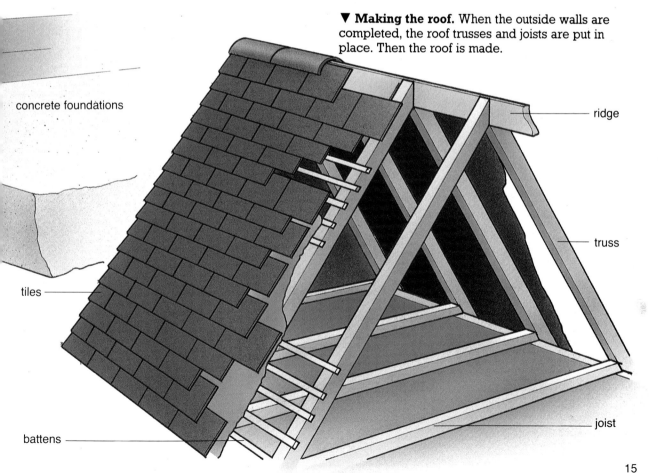

concrete foundations

ridge

truss

tiles

joist

battens

Water in the home

Each one of us uses many gallons of water in a day. We wash in it. We cook with it. We drink it. If we want water, we just turn on the tap. The water that comes from the mains is pure and safe to drink.

In many countries there are no water mains. People draw their water from wells or springs, or even from a river. This water is not always clear.

Our water supply

Our water supply comes from rainfall. The rain flows into streams and rivers. It is collected in water stores called **reservoirs**. Some reservoirs are very large. They can store enough water to supply a city for weeks or even months.

Water is pumped through underground mains to our homes from these reservoirs. The water we drink and cook with flows straight from the mains to the tap. More is piped to the cold tank in the roof. The cold tank is our own store of water for the home.

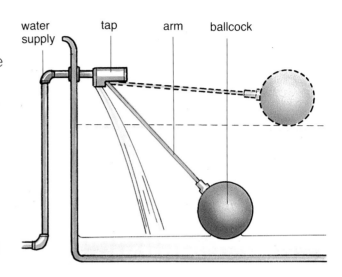

▲ A ballcock is a hollow plastic ball fixed to a long arm. The ball floats on the water. When the water level drops, the arm opens a tap and lets more water in. It closes the tap when the tank is nearly full.

The water supply in the house is controlled by taps and **ballcocks**. The ballcock cuts off the supply from the mains when the cold water tank is full. Taps let us draw off water when and where we want it.

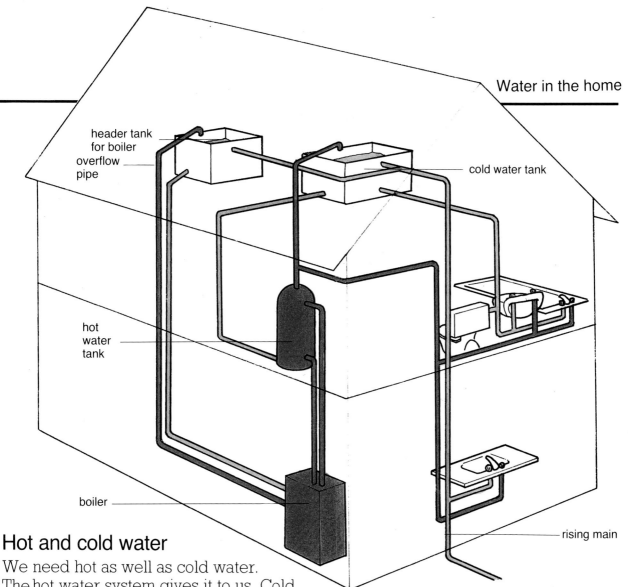

header tank
for boiler
overflow
pipe

cold water tank

hot
water
tank

boiler

rising main

Hot and cold water

We need hot as well as cold water.
The hot water system gives it to us. Cold
water is piped through a boiler. This
may burn oil, gas or solid fuel. It heats
the water which rises to the hot water
tank. As the hot water is used, more cold
water flows to the boiler to be heated.
Pipes lead from the hot water tank to
the hot taps.

Another way to heat water is by
electricity. An **immersion heater** is a
metal rod inside the hot water tank.
When the current is switched on, it heats
the rod. The heat passes into the water.
A switch cuts off the current before the
water boils.

▲ Cold water, marked blue, comes into your house
through the rising main. Hot water, red, is heated in
the boiler and rises to the hot water tank. There are
overflow pipes in case the water gets too hot in the
boiler, or in the hot water tank.

Drainage

We have to get rid of water that we have
used and made dirty. This is what drains
are for. They take away waste water
from our homes. Drains are linked to
sewer pipes in the street. All the waste
water from all the houses is piped away
to the **sewage** station. There, it is
pumped away, or cleaned and used again.

17

Power for the home

The main source of power in the home is electricity. It comes to us along mains cables from a power station. We use the current to light our homes and to help heat them. It can do the cooking and work machines in the kitchen. It provides power for TV and the radio.

There are three wires inside an electric cable. Two of these wires take the current from the power station to our homes and back again. The third is the ground wire. If there is any fault in the cable, the ground wire takes the current safely to ground.

▼ Look around your home. Make a list of all the things that use electricity.

Lights and heaters

Electric current passing through a wire makes heat. If the wire is thin, it will glow white hot. This is what happens in a light bulb. If the wire is thicker, it will get red hot. The wires in electric fires glow red. The thick wire of an electric fire uses more current than the thin wire of a light bulb.

Electricity is dangerous. Never play with it. Never switch lights off or on when your hands are wet. Never touch electric wires.

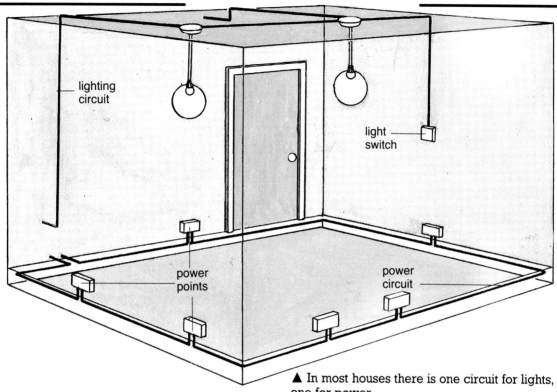

In the diagram: lighting circuit, light switch, power points, power circuit.

▲ In most houses there is one circuit for lights, and one for power.

An electric circuit

All the rooms in a house are linked up by electric wires. This network of wires is called a **circuit**. There is usually one circuit for the lights, and another one for the power points.

▼ Some electricity meters look like this one. Which pointer moves around the fastest?

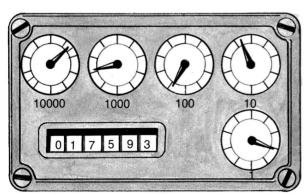

10000 1000 100 10

0 1 7 5 9 3

Lights and power points will work only if the circuit is complete. There must be two unbroken wires to carry the current. When we switch lights or power points off, we break the circuit. When you turn a switch off, it makes a gap in one or both of the wires. The current cannot jump the gap.

Measuring power

We have to pay for electricity. The more we use, the more we pay. A **meter** measures how much we use. There is a meter in every home. One type of meter has dials with pointers like the hands of a clock. When current is being used, the pointers move round. To save money and electricity, switch off lights when they are not being used.

Heating the home

We need energy to heat our homes, and for cooking. Most energy is produced by burning fuel. In some countries, wood or other fuel is burned on open fires. In others, homes are heated by electric or **central heating** systems.

There are some parts of the world where people do not need to heat their homes. The climate is warm enough all the year round. In these places, food is sometimes cooked in the open air.

Other places need heat for a large part of the year. Keeping a home warm also keeps it dry. Special care must be taken to keep young children and old people warm in cold weather.

▼ This picture shows the parts of a house where heat is lost. Can you think of good ways of saving energy?

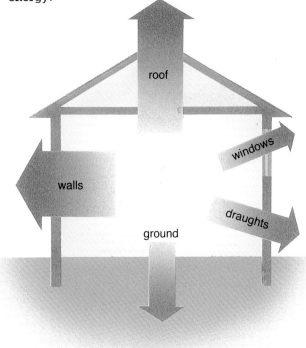

roof

windows

walls

draughts

ground

▲ In Kurdistan, people use animal dung as fuel. They store it in mounds under soil.

Losing heat

In cold weather, heat escapes from the house to the cold air outside. We save fuel if we can keep the heat in. This can be done by **insulation**.

In the roof space of some houses there is a thick layer of fiber or some other kind of insulation. Sometimes windows are **double-glazed**. They have an air space between two sheets of glass. Draught strips fitted to doors and windows also help to keep a house warm. Cavity walls can be fitted with plastic foam. This stops heat escaping through the walls. All these kinds of insulation help to keep heat in and fuel costs down.

How is your home heated?

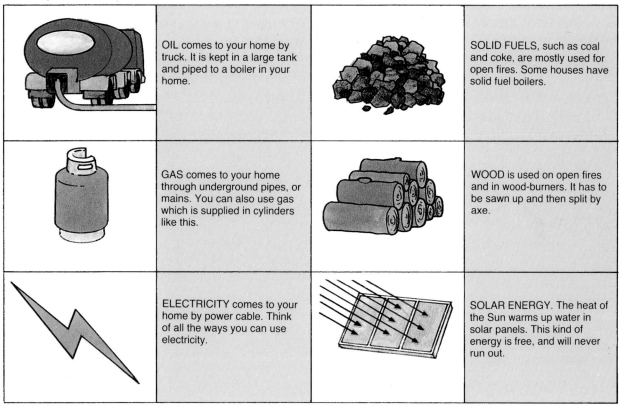

OIL comes to your home by truck. It is kept in a large tank and piped to a boiler in your home.

SOLID FUELS, such as coal and coke, are mostly used for open fires. Some houses have solid fuel boilers.

GAS comes to your home through underground pipes, or mains. You can also use gas which is supplied in cylinders like this.

WOOD is used on open fires and in wood-burners. It has to be sawn up and then split by axe.

ELECTRICITY comes to your home by power cable. Think of all the ways you can use electricity.

SOLAR ENERGY. The heat of the Sun warms up water in solar panels. This kind of energy is free, and will never run out.

Central heating

In a central heating system, hot water is pumped around a house through a boiler. The boiler burns oil, gas or solid fuel such as coal. Pipes lead from the boiler to **radiators** in each room. The same system gives hot water for baths and washing.

There are controls on oil and gas boilers. These can switch on and off at set times. They can switch off when a house is warm enough or switch on if it gets too cold. Each radiator can be turned on or off by hand. This prevents waste of energy in heating any rooms that are not in use.

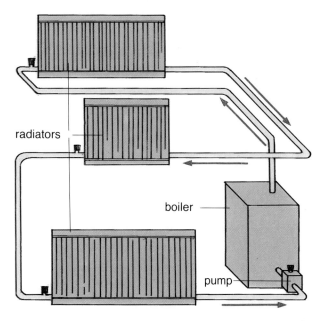

radiators

boiler

pump

In the kitchen

Modern kitchens are full of machines. Look around your own kitchen and see how many you can count. There are machines to store food and keep it cool. There are machines to help with cooking. Others wash dishes and clothes.

Most of these machines are electric. They save us time and work, but they all cost money to use.

Make sure that your hands are dry whenever you use an electric machine.

Electric kettle

An electric kettle boils water fast for making hot drinks. Inside the kettle is a ring of metal called a heating coil or **element**. When the kettle is switched on the element heats up. The heat is passed to the water. Some kettles switch themselves off when the water boils.

Electric motors

Electric current can be used to run a motor. A vacuum cleaner uses an electric motor to suck up dust. Many appliances in the kitchen have electric motors.

When the motor is switched on, the current makes a **coil** of wire turn. This is joined to a shaft. The shaft drives the machine.

Mixer

A mixer is a machine with an electric motor. When you make a cake, a mixer can be used to mix up the **ingredients**. It is easier and quicker to use a mixer than to do the mixing by hand. The shaft of the motor turns a set of blades. These make a smooth mixture.

Dishwasher

If you are lucky, you may have a dishwasher in your kitchen. All you have to do is to put the dirty dishes in and take them out when they are clean and dry. An electric element heats the water. A pump sprays hot water all over the dishes. More water rinses them. Finally the dishes are dried by hot air.

cooker

Washing machine

In most washing machines, the dirty clothes are put into a drum. Cold water is heated up. The drum spins to and fro, and hot water swishes through the washing. The dirty water is pumped away and clean water is pumped in. The clothes are dried by spinning, or by being shaken in warm air.

Refrigerator

A fridge (refrigerator) is a container which keeps food fresh and cool. It does this by pumping warmth out of the air. Inside the walls of the fridge there are pipes full of a cold liquid. This liquid is pumped through the pipes by a motor. As the liquid moves through the pipes, it takes away heat from the food.

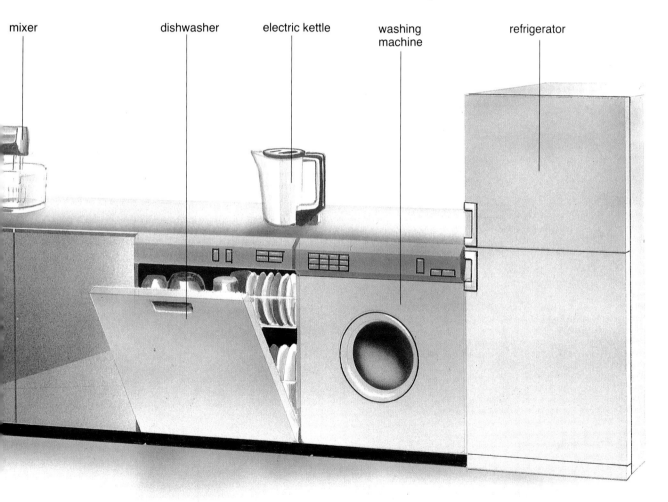

mixer | dishwasher | electric kettle | washing machine | refrigerator

Food and cooking

We can eat some foods raw, but most of our meals are cooked. Humans are the only animals that know how to cook food.

Cooking food changes it. It makes tough meat tender and easier to eat. Cooked food often tastes better, and our bodies can **digest** it more easily. The heat of cooking kills **bacteria** in the food. These are small germs that can make us ill. But the heat also takes away some of the goodness in food, so cooking time should be as short as possible.

How we cook food

There are many different ways of cooking. Think of potatoes. You can peel them and boil them in water. You can put potatoes in an oven and bake them with their skins on. Roasted potatoes are also cooked in an oven. You peel them first and give them a coating of fat. You can also slice potaotes and fry them in hot fat.

We all like the food that is grilled at a barbecue over a flame. Food can be cooked in a microwave oven in a few minutes. But the food does not get so brown as it does in a normal oven, or at a barbecue.

Fats

Fats are used a lot in preparing and cooking food. We need fats in our food to give us energy. The fat in our bodies helps us to keep warm in cold weather.

Fats come from animals and plants. Lard and butter are animal fats. Butter is made from the fat present in milk. It is made by shaking up, or **churning**, milk or cream. Churning separates the fat from the liquid. The fat becomes butter. Sometimes salt is added. You can make butter yourself by shaking up milk in a jar for about 20 minutes.

Cooking oils are fats that come from plants such as olives and coconuts. Margarine is also made from plant oils.

▲ Butter, milk and cream are rich in fats. They give us energy.

▲ Lemons and vinegar contain acid. They are used to flavor food and help us to digest it.

Keeping things clean

It is important to keep things clean in a kitchen. You should always wash your hands before handling food when you are cooking or eating.

The dishes used in cooking are often covered in a layer of fat. You cannot wash fat off with water alone. You need to add washing liquids, called **detergents**. These help the grease and water to mix so that the grease can be washed off.

Materials used in the home

Look around your home. You will see that all kinds of materials are used in it. Some, like wood, are natural. Others, like plastics, are man-made. There are all sorts of materials we can use. We choose some because they wear well. Others are easy to keep clean. We like to have some things in our homes that are good to look at.

How we use metal

Metal wears very well and lasts a long time. It stands up well to heat and is easy to keep clean.

Aluminum is lighter than most metals. It heats up quickly, so it is often used for saucepans, and for sinks. Copper is a soft metal that is easy to bend. It is often used for water pipes, and as electric wires.

Wood in the home

Wood can be cut and shaped. It can be polished or painted so that it is good to look at. Most chairs, beds and tables are made of wood. It is also used for doors, stairs and cupboards to put clothes in.

Wood burns easily and must be kept away from heat. It marks easily, and needs to be sealed or painted to keep it clean. This is why surfaces in the kitchen for chopping or cutting are often made of harder materials.

China

Most of the dishes we use at meals are made of china. China is made of a white clay. This is shaped and then baked in a kiln. Then the china is dipped in a liquid called glaze. When this is baked in the kiln again, it makes a glassy coating. The glaze makes it easy to keep china clean.

Plastics

Plastics are man-made. They can take the place of metal, wood and china in many ways. Look around your home and see how many things are made of plastics.

Some plastics can be bent and are **flexible**. We use flexible plastic bags to store food in the freezer. Other plastics are **rigid**. They cannot be bent. Kitchen surfaces are often made of rigid plastics. These stand up well to heat. They are easy to wipe down and keep clean.

▶ Look at the picture. Each of the colors stand for a different material. You can work out the materials for brown, pink, grey and yellow.

▼ Here are a few things made of plastic. Can you see any other plastic things in the room around you?

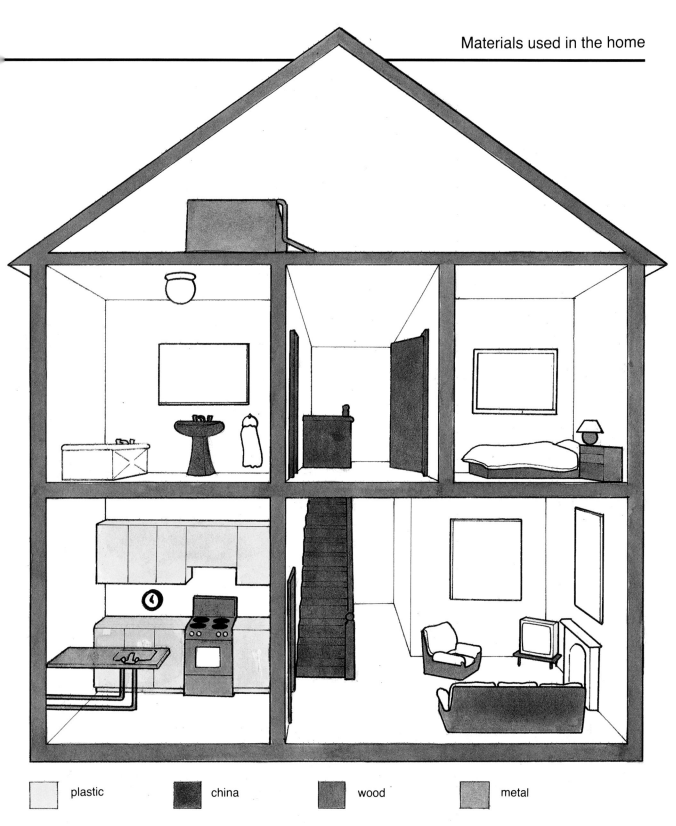

plastic   china   wood   metal

Fabrics in the home

Many things in your home are made of **fabrics**. Fabrics are made out of **fibers**. These are twisted together to make thread. Thread is woven to make fabrics.

Natural fibers come from plants and animals. Cotton comes from the cotton plant. Wool is the hair of sheep and other animals. There are also man-made fibers. These are made from chemicals. Each kind of fabric has different uses. The air trapped between the fibers of wool help to keep us warm. Clothes that are made of cotton are light and cool in hot weather. Man-made fabrics are easy to wash and they dry quickly.

▲ This is what wool fibers look like seen under a magnifying glass.

Spinning and weaving

Twisting fibers to make thread is called **spinning**. You can try this with a piece of cotton wool. Smooth and turn it in your fingers so that all the fibers point the same way. Damp your fingers. Twist the fibers between them. After a time you will have a piece of thread. Spinning machines work in the same way but twist the fibers more tightly.

Threads are woven by being passed over and under each other. You can see this if you look at a piece of fabric under a hand lens.

▼ You may wear clothes made of cotton or wool fabrics like these. Look closely at a garment you are wearing. You can see how the thread is woven.

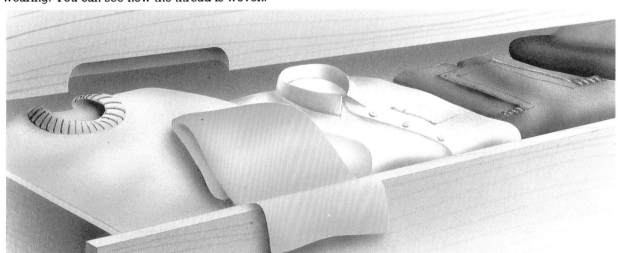

Man-made fibers

Nylon, polyester and rayon are three types of man-made fibers. They are made from carbon and other chemicals. The chemicals are melted. The liquid is sprayed from fine jets. The spray goes hard when it meets the air, and makes fibers. These can be spun like natural fibers.

Sometimes natural and man-made fibers are spun together. Mixed fibers give the fabrics the good points of both types. A sweater made of a mixture of wool and nylon will keep you warm. But it will be lighter and will dry quicker than one made of wool alone.

Using fabrics in the home

There are fabrics all around the house. Those used for curtains must hang well and look good. Chair covers have to be made from fabrics that will take hard wear. Sheets and blankets are made of fabrics that keep us warm in winter and cool in summer. The fabric used for towels is fluffy and thick. It has to soak up water.

Carpets are woven out of thread, like other fabrics. Some are made of wool alone. Many are made of mixed fibers. Some are made of man-made fibers only. Carpets have to take hard wear. They must still look good after many years.

▼ Make a list of all the different fabrics you can see in the picture, or in your own bedroom.

Keeping the home clean

There is always dust in the air around us. Dust is made up of tiny solid **particles**. They are small and light enough to float in the air. Some dust comes from the smoke of fires. Some is blown off the soil. The dust is so fine that we can easily breathe it in.

Dust on its own is not harmful. But it sometimes carries bacteria which cause disease. This is the main reason why we try to keep our homes clean and free of dust.

How does a vacuum cleaner work?

The best way to get rid of dust is to use a vacuum cleaner. Inside the cleaner is an electric motor. This drives a fan. The fan sucks air and dirt into a dust bag. A number of different tools can be fitted to the cleaner.

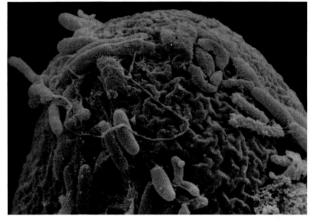

▲ Bacteria seen under a microscope. The real bacteria are hundreds of times smaller than in the picture.

The tool is passed over the surface to be cleaned. The fan sucks in air and dust. This goes into a bag that collects the dust. When the bag is full it is emptied or thrown away. An empty bag is put in its place.

▼ Inside a vacuum cleaner air is blown out by a fan. Air and dust rush in to fill the vacuum.

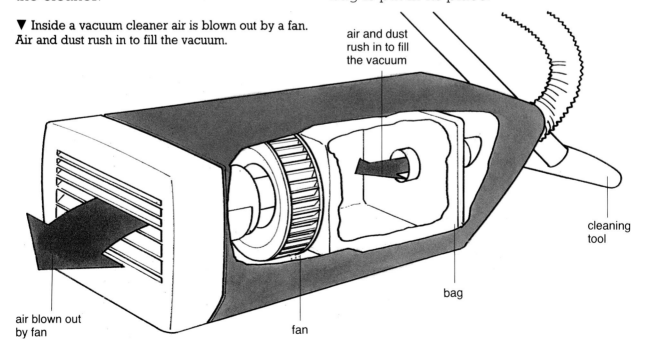

air and dust rush in to fill the vacuum

cleaning tool

bag

air blown out by fan

fan

▲ Many of the things at this rubbish dump can be recycled and used again.

Cleaning and polishing

Polishing things in the home keeps them clean. Polish contains oil or wax. When we polish something we leave a thin coat of oil or wax on it. This makes it shine. Polish removes dirt, stains and finger marks.

Metals such as brass and silver soon go dull if they are not kept polished. We say they **tarnish**.

Tarnish is a stain that comes from chemicals in the air. There are special metal polishes which remove it. Knives, spoons and forks are often made of stainless steel. This does not tarnish.

Where does rubbish go?

The dust and dirt that we clean up goes into the wastebasket. We also throw away old papers and other things that we no longer need. All these are taken away to a rubbish dump.

We throw away many things that could be used again. Glass and metal can be melted down and made into new things. Some of the paper that we throw away can be **recycled** to make new paper. If we could find an easy way to sort out our rubbish, less of it would have to be wasted.

How do telephones work?

▲ Sound waves are rather like the ripples made by a drop of rain falling on water.

When you speak, the sound of your voice is carried through the air. The sound spreads out in the air in all directions. Even if you shout, the sound of your voice cannot be heard very far away. It is soon lost.

Solid things carry sound better than air does. If you tap on a metal pipe in one part of your house, a friend can hear the sound easily in another part.

What is vibration?

When a sound is made it moves through the air and shakes it. Sound makes **vibrations**. The vibrations move outwards as waves. They are like the ripples you make when you throw a stone into a pond. Sound waves travel faster than ripples of water. Radio waves and electric current travel faster still.

Inside a telephone

Many people have telephones in their homes. You can use the phone to talk to friends in most parts of the world. A phone is connected to other phones by electric wires.

▼ With a modern phone you press the buttons to get a number instead of dialing.

The phone in your house has a handset. You pick this up when the phone rings or when you need to use it. The part of the handset that you put to your mouth is called the mouthpiece. Inside it there are small grains of carbon. An electric current passes through them. When you speak, your voice makes the grains of carbon vibrate. This makes changes in the current.

The current travels along the wires to your friend's phone. There is a cone of thin material in the earpiece of your friend's phone. The changes in the current from your voice make this cone vibrate. As you speak, the cone makes tiny movements all the time. These are heard as the sound of your voice.

Speaking to the world

Do you know your own phone number? Every phone in the world has a number. Each number is different. If you call from one country to another, you start by dialing that country's number. If you call long distance within the United States, you usually start by dialing one.

earpiece

small loudspeaker

mouthpiece

grains of carbon

You may know the phone numbers of some of your friends. What if you want to ring a friend whose number you do not know? Then you can use a **directory**. This is a book with names and numbers in it. It gives the numbers of all the people who live in one area.

33

Music for the home

We do not have to go to a concert each time we want to hear music. Sound recording gives us music in our own homes. We can choose what we want to hear. We can hear it as often as we like.

Recordings sound best on hi-fi systems. Hi-fi is short for high **fidelity**. This means that the recorded music sounds very much like live music.

There are three ways to listen to recorded music. One is on audio discs, or records. Another is on tape. The third way is on compact discs. These are the newest kind of recordings.

▼ How a record is made. Music is recorded on to a master tape. This is used to make a master disc.

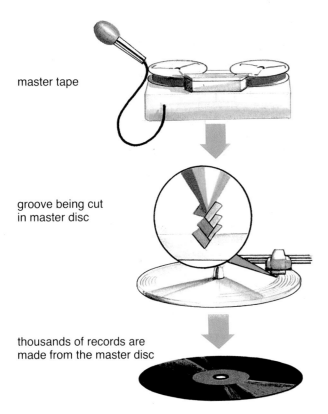

master tape

groove being cut in master disc

thousands of records are made from the master disc

▲ The music that you hear in your home has to be recorded in a studio like this one.

Recording music

Music is recorded in a studio. The instruments all make vibrations. These are picked up by microphones which change them into electric **signals**.

A number of microphones are used to record music. The signals from all of them are mixed to make the best sound. Then the signals are recorded on tape.

The tape is coated with tiny specks of metal. The electric signals arrange these in patterns. This stores the sound of the music on the tape. When the tape is played back, the signals are changed back into sound.

A master disc is made from the tape. The signals make a needle vibrate. The vibrations cut grooves in the master disc.

Stereo

At a live concert, there is sound all around you. **Stereo** gives you the same feeling in your home.

In stereo systems there are two loudspeakers. They are placed apart from each other. This helps you to pick out where the different instruments were at the time when the recording was made. This makes the recording sound more like live music.

Disc and tape

When we play a record, the **stylus** or needle picks up vibrations from the grooves in the disc. It changes these into

▲ A hi-fi system gives you stereo sound through two speakers. You can see one speaker on the left of the picture. You can play records on the turntable of the record player. You can play tapes on the tape deck. On some systems you can use compact discs. The system also has a tuner to pick up radio programs.

electric signals. The hi-fi system changes the signals into sounds.

Hi-fi systems may have cassette players. These give us sound from tape. The patterns of the tape are picked up by the tape head. This passes signals into the system. There they are changed into sound. The compact disc does not have grooves. Instead, the signals on the disc are 'read' by a laser beam.

Radio

Radios are very useful to us. We can carry them about. We can take them from room to room. Radio in a car helps us on long journeys. It gives us weather and traffic information, news and music.

Radio is sometimes called wireless. There are no wires bringing the sound to a radio set. The sound comes from signals that travel through the air.

What are radio waves?

The air is full of radio waves. You cannot see or feel them. Each radio station sends out its own pattern of waves. They are like the ripples on a pond. When the ripples are close together they are called short waves. When they are further apart they are long waves. The waves carry the signals to our radio sets.

Sending radio signals

Each radio station has a **transmitter**. This sends out radio waves from its **aerial**. The speech and music is changed into signals. These change the patterns of the waves. Some signals have a long way to travel to reach your set. The further the signals have to travel the weaker they become.

radio station

aerial

radio waves

◄ Many people have modern portable radios like this one. It has an aerial which you can extend. You can take the radio wherever you want to.

▼ Some busy people use car phones. They are linked to the exchange by radio.

▲ A radio program goes out from a radio station. The sounds of speech and music are changed into electric signals. These are transmitted as radio waves from a tall aerial. Your radio picks up these radio waves. It changes the waves back into speech and music.

Tuning in

Your radio set has a number of jobs to do. It must be able to pick out the station you want to hear from all the others. It does this when you turn the tuner. This picks out just one set of waves. Then the radio has to make the signal stronger. Finally the signal is changed back into sound.

Radio is also used so that people like the police can keep in touch with each other. These radios use short or very short waves.

Television and video

Television, like radio, comes to our homes on radio waves. The waves bring signals that give us the pictures as well as the sound. Wide bands of radio waves have to be used for TV. These are called channels.

TV signals can travel only a short way across the earth. The transmitter that gives you your TV shows has to be fairly close to your home.

The television camera

A TV camera is a kind of electric gun. It 'shoots' a current at the scene in front of it. It takes 25 pictures in each second.

Each picture is made up of thousands of dots of light. The camera changes light, shade and color into signals. Separate parts of the camera pick up the blue, red and green parts of the scene. All the colors you see on the screen are made up of mixtures of blue, red and green.

The signals from the camera are sent over wires to the transmitter. From there, they are sent out to viewers from the top of a high mast.

▼ A group of actors in a television studio.

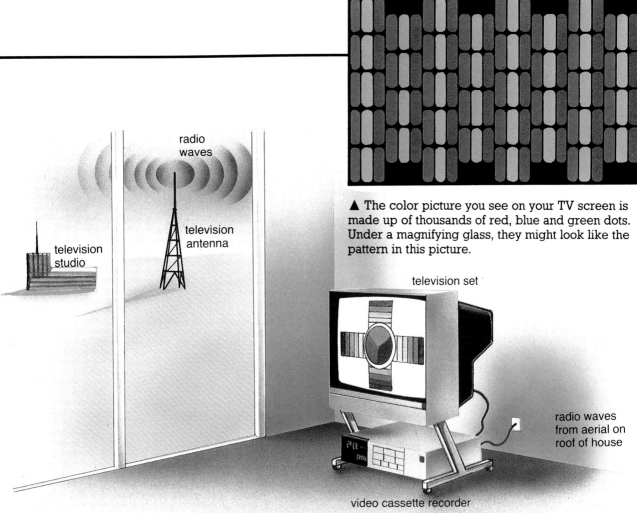

▲ The color picture you see on your TV screen is made up of thousands of red, blue and green dots. Under a magnifying glass, they might look like the pattern in this picture.

radio waves

television antenna

television studio

television set

radio waves from aerial on roof of house

video cassette recorder

▲ A TV program goes out from a studio. The pictures and sound go to the television antenna as electric signals. They go as radio waves from there to the aerial on the roof of your house. Your TV set turns the waves back into pictures and sound.

The television in your home

In your home, the TV signals are picked up by an aerial attached to the TV set. Like the camera, the set has a 'gun' which shoots electric currents. These currents carry the picture signals. They hit your TV screen at great speed. They light up blue, green or red specks on it. These points of light make up the picture. There are 25 pictures each second. A separate part of the TV set turns the sound signals back into sound. Cable television is a type of television system where the signals are sent by cable to the TV sets of viewers in their homes.

Video

A video cassette recorder plays TV films or programs which have been stored on tape. Videotape is like sound tape, but it is wider. It stores the picture and sound signals in the same way. Videos can record shows from our own TV sets. They can also show tapes that we can buy or hire to see on a TV set at home.

The home computer

A computer is a machine that stores and deals with information. It does the kind of work a human brain can do. Our brains store information in our memories. We can do things with this information. We can do sums, or put words in ABC order. We can arrange words to tell a story.

The computer also has a **memory**. It stores what we put into it. Then it can make use of the information. Computers can work much faster than the human brain. Computers are now so small that many people use them in their homes.

Input and output

Hardware is a word that is used for all the parts of a computer. There are three main parts. The **input** part is usually a keyboard. We can give commands or information to the computer through the keyboard. The computer unit itself is the second part. The third part is the **output**. This is what the computer tells us. It tells us by showing a message on a screen or printing it on paper. The message may give us the answer we want. If it cannot answer, it may ask us for more input.

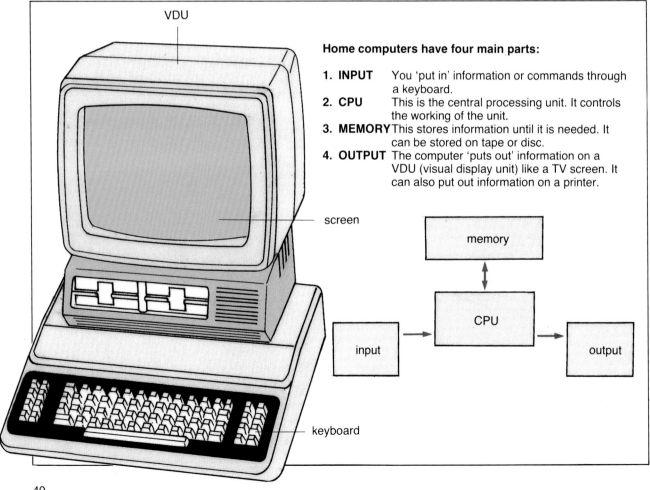

VDU

screen

keyboard

Home computers have four main parts:

1. **INPUT** You 'put in' information or commands through a keyboard.
2. **CPU** This is the central processing unit. It controls the working of the unit.
3. **MEMORY** This stores information until it is needed. It can be stored on tape or disc.
4. **OUTPUT** The computer 'puts out' information on a VDU (visual display unit) like a TV screen. It can also put out information on a printer.

memory

CPU

input

output

Giving commands

To give commands to a computer we have to use a special language on the keyboard. A computer cannot think for itself. We have to think for it. Each command has to be broken down into small steps. A set of commands is called a **program**. Programs are written in computer **language**. You must use the language that the computer can work with.

The **keyboard** of a computer is used in two ways. It can be used to give the computer information. It can be used to give it commands. The keys on the keyboard are pressed to make the computer print a message or show it on the screen.

▲ These children are having fun playing a computer game with each other.

Using computers at home

You can buy programs for computers or you can write your own. Programs are called **software**. There are programs for all kinds of uses.

Games are one kind of program. There are easy games for people still learning to use their computers. There are more difficult ones for experts. Computers are not toys. You can use them to learn new things. They can **store** information that you may need one day in the future. They can help people to manage their money or their business. One day you may have your own computer.

Homes in the future

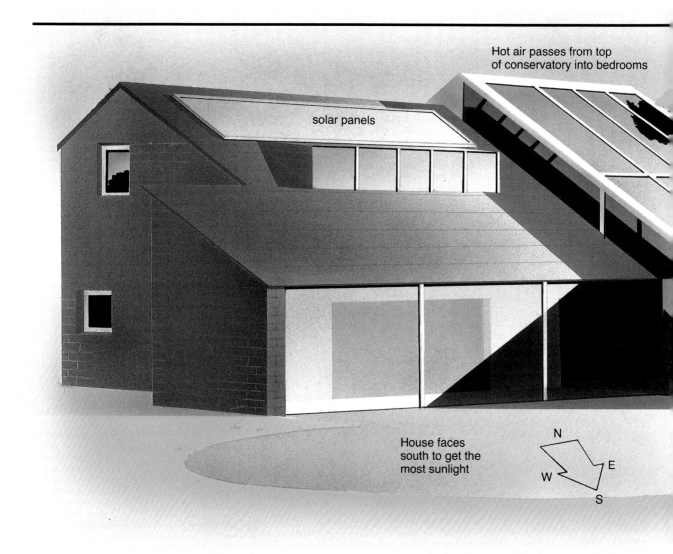

Hot air passes from top of conservatory into bedrooms

solar panels

House faces south to get the most sunlight

N
E
W
S

Winter in the northern countries of the world is cold. People have to heat their homes. Whatever kind of energy they use costs a lot of money.

In most houses, too much heat is wasted. It escapes through the walls, roof and floor. Too much heat goes up the chimney from the boiler into the open air. In the future, homes will be designed to keep the heat in better.

Saving energy

Insulation keeps heat in. It makes a barrier between the heat inside and the cold outside. Homes in the future will have more insulation than they have today. They will be made as airtight as possible. This will stop heat escaping through doors and walls. A thick layer of insulation will lie in the roof space. Thick blocks will insulate the walls.

Trees on east side to protect house from cold winds

Conservatory on east side of house. Can be used for growing food

Using Sun and glass

There is one source of heat that costs nothing. It is the Sun. All day, even if the Sun is not shining, it warms the Earth.

We can use the Sun's heat in two ways to warm our homes. One way is to fit **solar panels** to the roof. These can collect heat from the Sun and use it to heat water. The water stores the heat so that it can be used later.

The second way is to have more windows facing the Sun. These let the Sun's heat come into a house. This heat can be led away to the cooler parts of the house.

Facing the Sun

Builders in future will take more care in the way they place new houses. Solar panels have to face south in the northern part of the world. This way they catch the heat of the Sun. The roof facing the Sun will be large. There will be small windows and thick walls on the north side.

The house in the picture has a **conservatory** along the east wall of the house. This is used as an indoor garden for growing fruit and flowers. It becomes an extra room for people to sit in. The glass roof slopes towards the south.

The Sun's rays are trapped inside the conservatory. It becomes very warm inside. This insulates the east wall of the house. Some of the warm air can be led through the east wall into the bedrooms.

43

A robot in the home

Meet Zepo. He is a **robot**. He can move about. He can talk. He can do jobs, but he cannot think. He can only do things that he has been programmed to do.

Zepo moves on three wheels. When he goes upstairs two of these turn into legs which can bend. He has **sensors** instead of eyes. His sensors tell him to avoid bumping into things. He can pick up things with his arms and can turn his head.

Helping humans

Zepo is a friendly robot. He will not harm humans and will do as he is told. Zepo will protect himself and his home.

There are many jobs that Zepo could be trained to do. He could clean the house, wash the dishes, or even cook. Zepo could carry things for us. He could answer the door and keep strangers out.

Zepo can never be as clever as a human, because he cannot think for himself. He only knows what humans have put into his program. One day you might have a robot like Zepo in your own home!

Glossary

aerial: a radio or television antenna used for sending and receiving signals

architect: a person who plans new buildings

bacteria: very small living things, some of which cause disease

ballcock: a device for opening and closing the water supply to a tank. It is worked by a floating ball which rises and falls with the water level

batten: a long piece of wood used for fastening things to

cavity wall: a wall made up of two walls with a small gap between them

central heating: a form of heating in which a single source of heat is used to heat a building

chipboard: a wooden board made by gluing small pieces of wood together and then flattening them into a sheet

churn: to make butter by beating milk

circuit: the complete path of an electric current around a series of wires and connections

cladding: an outer covering

coil: a device made by winding wire round and round into a circular shape

community: a group of people who share things and help one another

concrete: a building material made from cement, sand, pebbles and water

conservatory: a room with glass walls and a glass roof, joined on to a house

design: a plan

detergent: a chemical substance used to remove dirt, oil or grease

digest: to break down food into simple substances which the body can use for growth and energy

directory: a list of names, addresses and telephone numbers

double-glazed: to have two sheets of glass in a window instead of one

earthquake: a sudden shaking or trembling of the Earth, which can cause buildings to collapse

element: the heating part of an electrical device

electricity: electrical energy

elevation: a drawing which shows the flat, upright side of a building

energy: the power to do work

fabric: any material made from natural or artificial fibers, like cotton, nylon or wool

fiber: a thin strand or thread

fidelity: closeness in sound

flexible: able to be bent without breaking

foundation: the solid base of a building, usually below the ground

generation: all the members of a family who are of a similar age

girder: a long, strong beam used to support the framework and floors of a building

hardware: the general name for all the parts of a computer

immersion heater: an electric water heater placed inside a water tank

ingredient: a part of a mixture

input: the commands and information which are fed into a computer

insulation: any process used to stop heat or sound from escaping or entering

insulator: any material through which heat or electricity will not pass

joist: one of the beams on which a floor is fixed

keyboard: the set of keys on the input part of a computer

language: a system of commands which are given to, and understood by, a computer

material: something from which other things can be made

memory: a store of information

meter: a device used for measuring how much of something has been used

mortar: a mixture of sand, lime and cement, which, when mixed with water, forms a material that dries hard

output: the information given out by a computer

particle: a small fragment of something

pitched: sloping

plan: a drawing which explains how a house should be built. A design

program: a set of instructions fed into a computer that makes it do a certain job or solve a problem

radiator: a device that gives out heat

rafter: one of the large beams that holds up a roof

recycle: to use something again

reservoir: a large tank or lake where water is stored before being used

rigid: stiff, not easy to bend

robot: a machine that can do tasks automatically once it has been programmed

sensor: a device that detects objects by sensing heat, light or sound

service: one of the main supplies, such as water or gas, which are connected to a house from a public system

sewage: waste material and liquid from houses, carried away by drains

shanty town: a town made up of badly built housing where the people live in poor conditions

signal: a sound, picture or message sent by an electrical impulse

site: a piece of ground for building on

software: the general term for computer programs, disks and cassettes

solar panel: a device that soaks up heat from the Sun. It is used to warm water

spinning: the making of thread by twisting a fiber such as wool or cotton

stereo: a sound system which gives out sound from two loudspeakers

store: keep

stylus: a needle-like device which picks up sound signals from a record

suburb: the outer area of a city, where people live

survey: to measure and inspect an area of land before building on it

tarnish: to become dull

technology: the science or study of engineering, or industrial skills; the use of science in industry

theodolite: an instrument used by surveyors to measure angles, so that an accurate plan can be drawn

transmitter: a device that sends out radio, television or electric signals

truss: a framework of beams used to support a roof

vibration: the action of moving to and fro or up and down very quickly